소리 내어 읽어 보는
30가지 이야기
── 초급 ──

Easy Korean
Reading
For Beginners

Easy Korean Reading For Beginners
소리 내어 읽어 보는 30가지 이야기 초급

1판1쇄	1st edition published	2018. 8. 1.
1판12쇄	12th edition published	2024. 4. 8.

지은이	Written by	TalkToMeInKorean
책임편집	Edited by	선경화 Kyung-hwa Sun, 에밀리 프리즈러키 Emily Przylucki
디자인	Designed by	김진영 Jinyoung Kim
삽화	Illustrations by	까나리 존스 Kanari Jones
녹음	Voice Recording by	TalkToMeInKorean
펴낸곳	Published by	롱테일북스 Longtail Books
펴낸이	Publisher	이수영 Su Young Lee
편집	Copy-edited by	김보경 Florence Kim
주소	Address	04033 서울특별시 마포구 양화로 113, 3층(서교동, 순흥빌딩)
		3rd Floor, 113 Yanghwa-ro, Mapo-gu, Seoul, 04033, KOREA
이메일	E-mail	TTMIK@longtailbooks.co.kr
ISBN	979-11-86701-93-5	13710

*이 교재의 내용을 사전 허가 없이 전재하거나 복제할 경우 법적인 제재를 받게 됨을 알려 드립니다.

*잘못된 책은 구입하신 서점이나 본사에서 교환해 드립니다.

TTMIK - TALK TO ME IN KOREAN

소리 내어 읽어 보는
30가지 이야기
—초급—

Easy Korean
Reading
For Beginners

written by **TalkToMeInKorean**

CONTENTS

Preface 6

How to Use This Book 7

1 요리 Cooking 9

2 영화 Movies 13

3 병원 Hospitals and Clinics 17

4 영화관 Movie Theaters 21

5 잠 Sleeping 25

6 편의점 Convenience Stores 29

7 쇼핑몰 Shopping Malls 33

8 버스 Buses 37

9 서점 Bookstores 41

10 동물원 The Zoo 45

11 캠핑 Camping 49

12 아침 시간 In the Morning 53

13 택배 Deliveries 57

14 안내 Information 61

15 회식 Company Dinners 65

16 생일 Birthdays 69

17 안내방송 Announcements 73

18 초대 Invitation 77

19 화장품 Makeup 81

20 편지 Letters 85

21 가을 Autumn 89

22 치매 Dementia 93

23 취미 Hobbies 97

24 소개 Introductions 101

25 반려동물 Pets 105

26 택시 Taxis 109

27 야식 Late-night Snacks 113

28 동호회 Clubs 117

29 핸드폰 Cell Phones 121

30 냉장고 Refrigerators 125

Preface

There is no doubt that reading is important and that finding the right reading material suitable for your level is also very important. If you look at most Korean reading texts and even storybooks for children, though, they are not meant for people who are learning Korean as a foreign language. That is why we have made this book for you.

Easy Korean Reading For Beginners provides you with bite-sized stories that are not overwhelming but are still effective in improving both your reading comprehension and vocabulary. Every story is presented with a comic strip to help you visualize the story in your head. We also give you pronunciation tips, translations, vocabulary information, and cultural tips.

Before you start reading more lengthy books such as short novels, children's storybooks, comic books, or webcomics, starting with Easy Korean Reading is a great way to give yourself more confidence in your Korean reading comprehension. Be sure to read everything out loud as you move through the book to check your pronunciation in comparison to the recordings by native speakers that are also available download on our website.

Now if you are ready, enjoy reading!

How to Use This Book

The title of each chapter shows what the following story will be about or where the following story will happen. There are 30 chapters in total, and each chapter has a different topic.

The illustration briefly depicts the plot of the story in a fun way. If there are new vocabulary words in the cartoon, footnotes are provided.

On the first page of each chapter, there is a short piece of writing without an English translation. Unless you are an absolute beginner, try reading it and guess what it means. Each chapter features a different style of writing, such as a letter, an announcement, an explanation, etc.

You can read the story in Korean out loud to practice your pronunciation. Words that are pronounced differently than the way they are spelled are highlighted in the pronunciation keys.

The translation of the story is on the third page of the chapter. Compare line by line to check if you understood the meaning correctly.

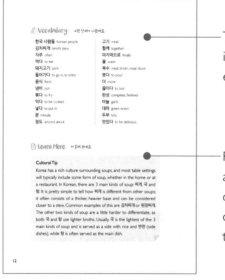

The vocabulary words introduced in the story are on the last page of each chapter.

Finally, if you want to learn more about the topic of the chapter, you can read an interesting cultural tip or learn more related vocabulary at the end of each chapter.

01

요리 cooking

한국 사람들은 김치찌개를 자주 먹어요. 김치찌개에는 김치와 돼지고기가 들어가요. 먼저, 냄비에 돼지고기를 넣고 볶아요. 그리고 돼지고기가 익으면 김치를 넣어요. 3분 정도 고기와 김치를 함께 볶아요. 마지막으로, 물이나 육수를 붓고 더 끓이면 완성이에요. 마늘, 대파, 두부를 넣으면 더 맛있어요.

* 치익 치익: The sound of putting meat on a hot grill ** 넘치다: to overflow

[사람드른]　　　　　　　　　　[머거요]
한국 **사람들**은 김치찌개를 자주 **먹어요**.

　　　　　　　　　　　　　　[드러가요]
김치찌개에는 김치와 돼지고기가 **들어가요**.

　　　　　　　　　[너코] [보까요]
먼저, 냄비에 돼지고기를 **넣고 볶아요**.

　　　　　　　　　[이그면]　　　[너어요]
그리고 돼지고기가 **익으면** 김치를 **넣어요**.

[삼분]　　　　　　　　　　　　[보까요]
3분 정도 고기와 김치를 함께 **볶아요**.

[마지마그로]　[무리나] [육쑤를] [붇꼬]　　[끄리면]
마지막으로, **물이나 육수를** 붓고 더 **끓이면** 완성이에요.

　　　　　　　　　[너으면]　　　[마시써요]
마늘, 대파, 두부를 **넣으면** 더 **맛있어요**.

Koreans often eat kimchi stew.

There is kimchi and pork in kimchi stew.

First, put the pork into a pot and fry it.

When the pork is cooked, add the kimchi.

Fry the pork and the kimchi together for approximately 3 minutes.

Finally, pour in some water or broth and boil it some more, then it's done.

If you add garlic, scallions, and tofu, it's even tastier.

✏ Vocabulary 이런 단어가 나왔어요

- 한국 사람들 Korean people
- 김치찌개 kimchi stew
- 자주 often
- 먹다 to eat
- 돼지고기 pork
- 들어가다 to go in, to enter
- 음식 food
- 냄비 pot
- 볶다 to fry
- 익다 to be cooked
- 넣다 to put in
- 분 minute
- 정도 around, about

- 고기 meat
- 함께 together
- 마지막으로 finally
- 물 water
- 육수 meat broth, meat stock
- 붓다 to pour
- 더 more
- 끓이다 to boil
- 완성 complete, finished
- 마늘 garlic
- 대파 green onion
- 두부 tofu
- 맛있다 to be delicious

📄 Learn More 더 읽어 보세요

Cultural Tip

Korea has a rich culture surrounding soups, and most table settings will typically include some form of soup, whether in the home or at a restaurant. In Korean, there are 3 main kinds of soup: 찌개, 국 and 탕. It is pretty simple to tell how 찌개 is different from other soups; it often consists of a thicker, heavier base and can be considered closer to a stew. Common examples of this are 김치찌개 or 된장찌개. The other two kinds of soup are a little harder to differentiate, as both 국 and 탕 use lighter broths. Usually, 국 is the lightest of the 3 main kinds of soup and is served as a side with rice and 반찬 (side dishes), while 탕 is often served as the main dish.

02

영화 Movies

영화 '부산행'을 봤어요. 이 영화는 연상호 감독의 좀비 영화예요. 이 영화는 연상호 감독이 처음으로 만든 실사 영화예요. 이 감독은 이 영화를 만들기 전에는 항상 애니메이션을 만들었어요. 그 애니메이션 영화들이 너무 좋아서, 이번에 새로운 영화에 대해서 기대를 많이 했어요. 저는 원래 좀비 영화를 좋아하지 않아요. 그런데 이 영화는 정말 재미있었어요.

* 돼지의 왕, 사이비: Sang-ho Yeon's previous animated films, called "The King of Pigs" and "The Fake" in English. ** 재밌겠다: This is going to be fun. *** 으악: The sound you make when you are surprised

[봐써요]
영화 '부산행'*을 **봤어요**.

[감두긔 or 감도게]
이 영화는 연상호 **감독의** 좀비 영화예요.

[감도기] [처으므로]　　[실싸]
이 영화는 연상호 **감독이 처음으로** 만든 **실사** 영화예요.

[감도근]　　　　　　　　[저네는]　　[애니메이셔늘] [만드러써요]
이 **감독은** 이 영화를 만들기 **전에는** 항상 **애니메이션을 만들었어요**.

[영화드리]　　[조아서]　[이버네]
그 애니메이션 **영화들이** 너무 **좋아서, 이번에** 새로운 영화에 대해서
[마니] [해써요]
기대를 **많이 했어요**.

[월래]　　　　　　[조아하지] [아나요]
저는 **원래** 좀비 영화를 **좋아하지 않아요**.

[재미이써써요]
그런데 이 영화는 정말 **재미있었어요**.

* 부산행 is pronounced as 부사냉 when you say it quickly.

I saw the movie "Train to Busan".

This movie is a zombie film by director Sang-ho Yeon.

This movie is director Sang-ho Yeon's first live-action movie.

Before making this movie, the director always made animations.

I liked his animated movies so much, so I was very excited about this new movie.

I usually don't like zombie movies.

However this movie was really fun.

✏ Vocabulary 이런 단어가 나왔어요

- 영화 movie
- 보다 to watch
- 감독 director
- 좀비 zombie
- 처음으로 for the first time
- 만들다 to make
- 실사 live action
- 전 before
- 항상 always
- 좋다 to like, to be good
- 새롭다 to be new

- 기대하다 to look forward to
- 정말 really
- 재미있다 to be fun

📄 Learn More 더 읽어 보세요

Jobs Related to Movies
영화 감독 movie director
촬영 감독 cinematographer
음향 감독 musical director
미술 감독 art director
조명 감독 lighting director
캐스팅 디렉터 casting director
영화 제작자 film producer
작가 writer
영화배우 actor
영화 평론가 movie critic

03

병원 Hospitals and Clinics

배가 너무 아파요. 그래서 집 근처에 있는 병원에 가요. 병원에 가면 먼저, 접수를 해야 해요. 이름과 주소, 전화번호를 적어요. 그다음에 대기실에서 기다려요. 간호사가 이름을 불러요. 의사 선생님이 진찰을 해요. 주사를 맞아요. 처방전을 받고 약국에 가요. 약을 받아요. 집에 가서 약을 먹고 쉬어요.

---

* 주사는 꼭 맞아야 해요?: Should I really get an injection? ** 하나도 안 아파요 걱정 마세요: It doesn't hurt at all. Don't worry.

[인는] [병워네]
배가 너무 아파요. 그래서 집 근처에 **있는 병원에** 가요.

[병워네]   [접쑤를]
병원에 가면 먼저, **접수를** 해야 해요.

[저거요] [그다으메] [대기시레서]
이름과 주소, 전화번호*를 **적어요. 그다음에 대기실에서** 기다려요.

[이르믈]
간호사*가 **이름을** 불러요.

[선생니미] [진차를]
의사 **선생님이 진찰을** 해요.

[마자요] [처방저늘] [받꼬] [약꾸게]
주사를 **맞아요. 처방전을 받고 약국에** 가요.

[야글] [바다요]
약을 받아요.

[지베]   [야글] [먹꼬]
집에 가서 **약을 먹고** 쉬어요.

---

* 전화번호 and 간호사 are pronounced as 저놔버노 and 가노사 when you say them quickly.

My stomach hurts so much. So I go to the clinic near my house.

When I go to the clinic, I have to sign in first.

I write my name, address, and phone number. Then I wait in the waiting room.

The nurse calls my name.

The doctor examines me.

I get an injection. I get a prescription and go to the pharmacy.

I get some medicine.

I go home, take the medicine, and rest.

✎ Vocabulary 이런 단어가 나왔어요

- 배 stomach
- 너무 too much, very
- 아프다 to ache, to hurt, to be sick
- 집 house, home
- 근처 near, nearby
- 병원 hospital, clinic
- 가다 to go
- 접수 application
- 이름 name
- 주소 address
- 전화번호 phone number
- 적다 to write down
- 대기실 waiting room
- 기다리다 to wait

- 간호사 nurse
- 부르다 to call
- 의사 선생님 doctor
- 진찰을 하다 to examine
- 주사 injection, shot
- 주사를 맞다 to get an injection
- 처방전 prescription
- 받다 to receive
- 약국 pharmacy
- 가다 to go
- 약 medicine
- 먹다 to eat
- 쉬다 to rest

📄 Learn More 더 읽어 보세요

Types of Hospitals
대학 병원 university hospital
종합 병원 general hospital
내과 department of internal medicine
외과 department of surgery
이비인후과 otolaryngology, ear-nose-and-throat department
안과 department of ophthalmology
소아과 pediatric department
산부인과 ob/gyn, obstetrics, gynecology department

04

영화관 Movie Theaters

친구랑 영화를 볼 거예요. 저는 무서운 영화를 좋아해요. 그런데 제 친구는 무서운 영화를 싫어해요. 그래서 그냥 액션 영화를 볼 거예요. 이 영화는 인기가 정말 많아요. 그래서 어제 미리 표를 샀어요. 영화를 보기 전에 팝콘이랑 콜라를 샀어요. 영화가 곧 시작될 거예요. 너무 기대돼요.

---

* 공포 영화: horror movie ** 쳇: Hmph. *** 으앙: The sound people make when they cry

[볼 꺼예요]
친구랑 영화를 **볼 거예요**.

[조아해요]
저는 무서운 영화를 **좋아해요**.

[시러해요]
그런데 제 친구는 무서운 영화를 **싫어해요**.

[액쎤]　　　[볼 꺼예요]
그래서 그냥 **액션** 영화를 **볼 거예요**.

[인끼가]　　　[마나요]
이 영화는 **인기가** 정말 **많아요**.

[사써요]
그래서 어제 미리 표를 **샀어요**.

[저네] [팝코니랑]　　[사써요]
영화를 보기 **전에 팝콘이랑** 콜라를 **샀어요**.

[시작뙬 꺼예요]
영화가 곧 **시작될 거예요**. 너무 기대돼요.

I'm going to watch a movie with my friend.

I like scary movies.

However my friend hates scary movies.

So we will just watch an action movie.

This movie is really popular.

So, I bought the ticket in advance yesterday.

I bought popcorn and a cola before we watch the movie.

The movie will start soon. I'm looking forward to it.

✎ Vocabulary 이런 단어가 나왔어요

- 친구 friend
- 영화 movie
- 보다 to watch
- 무섭다 to be scary
- 좋아하다 to like
- 싫어하다 to hate, to dislike
- 인기가 많다 to be popular
- 어제 yesterday
- 미리 already, beforehand
- 표 ticket
- 사다 to buy
- 전 before
- 팝콘 popcorn
- 콜라 Coke, cola

- 곧 soon
- 시작되다 to start
- 기대되다 to look forward to

📄 Learn More 더 읽어 보세요

Types of Movies/Films

공포 영화 horror movie

멜로 영화 romantic movie

액션 영화 action movie

전쟁 영화 war movie

코미디 영화 comedy movie

SF 영화 (공상과학 영화) science fiction movie

애니메이션 animation, animated movie

드라마 drama movie

가족 영화 family movie

05

잠 Sleeping

잠을 푹 자는 것은 정말 중요해요. 잠이 잘 안 오면 이런 방법을 써 보세요. 1. 매일 같은 시간에 잠을 자고 같은 시간에 일어나세요. 2. 낮에 가벼운 운동을 해 보세요. 3. 자기 전에 심한 운동은 하지 마세요. 4. 저녁에는 커피나 녹차, 홍차 같은 카페인이 있는 음료는 피하세요. 5. 저녁에 음식을 너무 많이 먹지 마세요. 6. 자기 전에 따뜻한 우유를 한 잔 드세요.

* 달인: master ** 카: The sound people make after drinking something, especially alcohol

[자물]　　　　[거슨]
잠을 푹 자는 **것은** 정말 중요해요.

[자미]　　[아 노면]　　　[방버블]
잠이 잘 **안 오면** 이런 **방법을** 써 보세요.

　　　　　[가튼] [시가네] [자물]　　　[기튼] [시가네] [이러나세요]
1. 매일 **같은 시간에 잠을** 자고 **같은 시간에 일어나세요.**

　　　[나제]
2. **낮에** 가벼운 운동을 해 보세요.

　　　　[저네]
3. 자기 **전에** 심한* 운동은 하지 마세요.

　　　[저녀게는]　　　　　　　　　[가튼] [카페이니] [인는] [음뇨는]
4. **저녁에는** 커피나 녹차, 홍차 **같은 카페인이 있는 음료는** 피하세요.

　　　[저녀게] [음시글]　　　[마니] [먹찌]
5. **저녁에** 음식을 너무 **많이 먹지** 마세요.

　　　　[저네] [따뜨탄]
6. 자기 **전에 따뜻한** 우유를 한 잔 드세요.

* 심한 is pronounced as 시만 when you say it quickly.

It is really important to sleep well.

If you cannot sleep, try this method.

1. Go to sleep at the same time and get up at the same time every day.

2. Try doing some light exercise during the day.

3. Do not do intense exercise right before you go to bed.

4. Avoid caffeinated beverages such as coffee, green tea, or black tea in the evening.

5. Do not eat too much food in the evening.

6. Have a glass of warm milk before you go to bed.

- 잠 sleep
- 푹 (자다) (to sleep) well
- 자다 to sleep
- 정말 really
- 중요하다 to be important
- 이런 this, such
- 방법 method
- 쓰다 to use
- 매일 every day
- 같은 same
- 시간 time
- 일어나다 to wake up
- 낮 day, daytime
- 가볍다 to be light

- 운동 exercise
- 심하다 to be harsh, to be severe, to be intense
- 저녁 evening
- 녹차 green tea
- 홍차 black tea
- 카페인 caffeine
- 음료 beverage
- 피하다 to avoid
- 많이 a lot, many, much
- 먹다 to eat
- 따뜻하다 to be warm
- 우유 milk
- 잔 numerical counter for cups or glasses
- 들다 to eat, to drink (honorific)

Learn More 더 읽어 보세요

Expressions Related to Sleeping

잠옷 pajamas, sleepwear
베개 pillow
침실 bedroom
잠을 자다 to sleep
알람을 맞추다 to set the alarm
이불을 펴다 to make the bed, to lay out the bedding (on the floor)
이불을 덮다 to cover oneself with blankets/bedding, to tuck into bed
불을 끄다 to turn off the light
잠꼬대를 하다 to talk in one's sleep
코를 골다 to snore
뒤척이다 to toss and turn
잠을 설치다 to have a restless night's sleep, to not sleep well
잠에서 깨다 to awake from sleep

이불 blanket, covers, comforter
침대 bed
알람시계 alarm clock
하품하다 to yawn

눕다 to lie down
꿈을 꾸다 to dream
이를 갈다 to grind one's teeth

06

편의점 Convenience Stores

요즘 편의점 음식이 인기가 많아요. 편의점에서는 음료수랑 과자도 팔고, 김밥과 과일도 팔아요. 그리고 도시락도 팔아요. 편의점 도시락은 가격도 싸고 종류도 다양해요. 그래서 점심으로 편의점 도시락을 먹는 사람들이 많아요.

* 전자레인지에 데워 먹자: Let's warm it up in the microwave before we eat it. ** 간편하고 맛도 좋아: It's convenient and tasty.

[음시기] [인끼가] [마나요]
요즘 **편의점 음식이 인기가 많아요.**
　[펴늬점 or 펴니점]

[음뇨수랑]　　　　　　[김빱꽈]　　　　[파라요]
편의점에서는 음료수랑 과자도 팔고, **김밥과** 과일도 **팔아요.**
[펴늬저메서는 or 펴니저메서는]

[도시락또] [파라요]
그리고 **도시락도 팔아요.**

[도시라근] [가격또]　　[종뉴도]
편의점 도시락은 가격도 싸고 **종류도** 다양해요.
[펴늬점 or 펴니점]

[점시므로]　　　　[도시라글] [멍는] [사람드리] [마나요]
그래서 **점심으로 편의점 도시락을 먹는 사람들이 많아요.**
　　　　[펴늬점 or 펴니점]

These days, convenience store food is really popular.

At the convenience store, they sell soft drinks and snacks, and they also sell kimbap and fruit.

They also sell lunch boxes.

Convenience store lunch boxes are cheap and there are various kinds.

So, there are many people who eat lunch boxes from convenience stores for lunch.

✐ Vocabulary 이런 단어가 나왔어요

- 요즘 these days
- 편의점 convenience store
- 음식 food
- 인기가 많다 to be popular
- 음료수 beverage
- 과자 snack
- 과일 fruit
- 도시락 lunch box
- 팔다 to sell
- 가격 price
- 싸다 to be cheap
- 종류 kind, type
- 다양하다 to be various
- 점심 lunch

- 먹다 to eat
- 사람들 people
- 많다 to be a lot

📄 Learn More 더 읽어 보세요

Types of Stores
백화점 department store, mall
슈퍼마켓 grocery store
구멍가게 small store, mom-and-pop store
편의점 convenience store
마트 warehouse store, big-box store
쇼핑몰 shopping mall, shopping center
아웃렛 outlet store, outlet mall

07

쇼핑몰 Shopping Malls

한국에는 큰 쇼핑몰이 많아요. 쇼핑몰에 가면 할 수 있는 게 정말 많아요. 옷 가게에서 쇼핑도 할 수 있어요. 음식점에서 식사도 할 수 있어요. 영화관에서 영화도 볼 수 있어요. 요즘 새로 생긴 쇼핑몰에는 수영장도 있고 찜질방도 있어요. 비가 오거나 날씨가 추울 때는 쇼핑몰에 사람이 정말 많아요.

* 안: inside ** 앞: the front *** 영화관으로 와: Come to the movie theater.

[한구게는]　　[쇼핑모리]　[마나요]
한국에는 큰 **쇼핑몰이** **많아요.**

[쇼핑모레]　　　[할 쑤] [인는]　　　　[마나요]
쇼핑몰에 가면 **할 수 있는** 게 정말 **많아요.**

[온 까게에서]　　　　[할 쑤] [이써요]
옷 가게에서 쇼핑도 **할 수 있어요.**

[음식쩌메서] [식싸도] [할 쑤] [이써요]
음식점에서 **식사도** **할 수 있어요.**

[영화과네서]　　　　[볼 쑤] [이써요]
영화관에서 영화도 **볼 수 있어요.**

[쇼핑모레는]　　　　[읻꼬]　　　[이써요]
요즘 새로 생긴 **쇼핑몰에는** 수영장도 **있고** 찜질방도 **있어요.**

[쇼핑모레] [사라미]　　[마나요]
비가 오거나 날씨가 추울 때는 **쇼핑몰에** **사람이** 정말 **많아요.**

There are many big shopping malls in Korea.

There are so many things you can do when you go to a shopping mall.

You can shop at a clothes store.

You can eat at a restaurant.

You can watch a movie in the movie theater.

These days, in the newer shopping malls, there are even swimming pools and spas.

When it rains or the weather is cold, there are so many people at the mall.

- 한국 Korea
- 크다 to be big
- 쇼핑몰 shopping mall
- 많다 to be a lot
- 옷 clothes
- 가게 store
- 쇼핑 shopping
- 음식점 restaurant
- 식사 meal
- 영화관 movie theater
- 영화 movie

- 보다 to watch
- 요즘 these days
- 새로 new, newer
- 생기다 to open
- 수영장 swimming pool
- 찜질방 Korean dry sauna
- 비가 오다 to rain
- 날씨 weather
- 춥다 to be cold
- 사람 person
- 정말 really

📄 Learn More   더 읽어 보세요

Cultural Tip

In Korea, a popular kind of sauna is called 찜질방. 찜질방s are usually large buildings with separate areas for men and women. You receive clothing and towels at the front desk, then go into the gender-appropriate locker rooms where you can change clothes and store personal items. Also in these gender-specific areas, there are large bathing rooms but you must undress before going in. In this area, you can do many things: bathe in hot and cold pools, take a shower, get a massage or scrub, or sit in different kinds of saunas. After bathing, you put on your sauna clothes and head up to the gender-neutral space where you can sit in dry saunas, watch TV, sleep, or order snacks from the snack bar. Many 찜질방s also have reading rooms, game rooms, computer rooms, and even singing rooms in the shared area! If you're tired, you can even spend the night; the shared area has sleeping mats and pillow blocks for your convenience.

08

버스 Buses

버스는 대중교통 수단 중 하나예요. 여러 사람이 같이 탈 수 있어요. 버스는 정류장에만 서요. 그래서 버스를 타고 싶으면 버스 정류장에서 기다려야 해요. 버스가 도착하면, 앞문으로 타요. 그리고 내릴 때는 뒷문으로 내려요. 한국에서는 버스 요금이 천 원 정도예요. 버스에서 내리고 싶으면 미리 벨을 눌러야 해요.

---

* 끼익: The sound of a car stopping suddenly (the sound of a vehicle braking) ** 현금: cash *** 출퇴근 시간은 붐벼요: It's crowded during rush hour.

[뻐쓰는]
버스는 대중교통 수단 중 하나예요.

[사라미] [가치] [탈 쑤] [이써요]
여러 **사람이 같이 탈 수 있어요.**

[뻐쓰는] [정뉴장에만]
버스는 정류장에만 서요.

[뻐쓰를] [시프면] [뻐쓰] [정뉴장에서]
그래서 **버스를** 타고 **싶으면 버스 정류장에서** 기다려야 해요.

[뻐쓰가] [도차카면] [암무느로]
버스가 도착하면, 앞문으로 타요.

[뒨무느로]
그리고 내릴 때는 **뒷문으로** 내려요.

[한구게서는] [뻐쓰] [요그미] [처 눤]
한국에서는 버스 요금이 천 원 정도예요.

[뻐쓰에서] [시프면] [베를]
버스에서 내리고 **싶으면** 미리 **벨을** 눌러야 해요.

Buses are one means of public transportation.

Several people can ride together.

Buses only stop at bus stops.

So if you want to take the bus, you have to wait at the bus stop.

When the bus arrives, get on through the front door.

When you get off, get off through the back door.

In Korea, the bus fare is about 1,000 won.

If you want to get off the bus, you have to press the bell in advance.

✐ Vocabulary 이런 단어가 나왔어요

- 버스 bus
- 대중교통 transportation
- 수단 means, way
- 여러 many, several
- 사람 person
- 같이 together
- 타다 to ride
- 정류장 stop, station
- 서다 to stop
- 타다 to ride
- 기다리다 to wait

- 도착하다 to arrive
- 앞문 front door
- 내리다 to get off
- 뒷문 rear door
- 요금 fare, charge
- 천원 1,000 won
- 정도 about, around
- 미리 beforehand, in advance
- 벨 bell
- 누르다 to press, to push

📄 Learn More 더 읽어 보세요

Cultural Tip

The bus system in Korea, particularly in Seoul, is well-developed and convenient. There are different kinds of buses that you can take, such as inter-city, intra-city, airport buses, village buses, and express buses. The buses are color-coded so that you can tell at a glance which kind of bus it is. Inter-city buses and airport buses are usually maroon, dark blue, or dark red. Red buses go to more suburban areas farther outside the city. Blue and green buses are intra-city buses that travel between subway stations; blue buses travel longer distances than green ones. Yellow buses make roundabouts in downtown Seoul around the main shopping and business locations. There are also village buses which are often colored yellow or green that operate within specific districts, but don't worry; you won't get them confused with the other green and yellow buses because they are much smaller!

09

서점 Bookstores

저는 가끔 서점에 가요. 서점에 가면 먼저, 베스트셀러 책들을 확인해요. 그러고 나서 새로 나온 책들을 확인해요. 저는 주로 소설을 읽어요. 요즘에는 추리 소설을 읽고 있어요. 저는 책을 사기 전에 조금 읽어 보는 걸 좋아해요. 그래서 큰 서점에 가요. 큰 서점에서는 의자에 앉아서 책을 읽을 수 있어요.

---

* 마니아: a huge fan ** 스윽: The motion of someone moving slowly and secretly (elongated for effect) *** 소곤소곤: The sound or motion of whispering

[서저메]
저는 가끔 **서점에** 가요.

[서서메]　　　　　　[베스트쎌러] [책뜨를] [화긴해요]
서점에 가면 먼저, **베스트쎌러 책들을 확인해요**＊.

　　　　　　　　　　[책뜨를] [화긴해요]
그러고 나서 새로 나온 **책들을 확인해요**＊.

　　　　　[소서를] [일거요]
저는 주로 **소설을 읽어요**.

[요즈메는]　　　[소서를] [일꼬] [이써요]
요즘에는 추리 **소설을 읽고 있어요**.

　　　[채글]　　[저네]　　[일거]　　　　[조아해요]
저는 **책을** 사기 **전에** 조금 **읽어** 보는 걸 **좋아해요**.

　　　　　[서저메]
그래서 큰 **서점에** 가요.

　　　[서저메서는]　　　　　[안자서] [채글] [일글 쑤] [이써요]
큰 **서점에서는** 의자에 **앉아서 책을 읽을 수 있어요**.

＊ 확인해요 is pronounced as 화기내요 when you say it quickly.

I sometimes go to the bookstore.

When I go to the bookstore, first I check out the bestselling books.

Then I check out the new books.

I usually read novels.

I'm reading a mystery novel these days.

I like reading a little before buying a book.

So I go to big bookstores.

In a big bookstore, you can sit in a chair and read books.

✎ Vocabulary   이런 단어가 나왔어요

- 가끔 often
- 서점 bookstore
- 가다 to go
- 먼저 first
- 베스트 셀러 bestseller
- 책 book
- 확인하다 to check, to see
- 새로 new
- 나오다 to be published
- 주로 mainly, mostly
- 소설 novel

- 읽다 to read
- 요즘 these days
- 추리 소설 mystery story, detective novel
- 조금 a little
- 좋아하다 to like
- 크다 to be big
- 의자 chair
- 앉다 to sit

📄 Learn More   더 읽어 보세요

Types of Books

소설 novel

수필 essay

시 poem

동화책 fairy tale book

자서전 autobiography

자기계발서 self-improvement book

요리책 recipe book

위인전 biography (of a great person)

교과서 textbook

문제집 workbook

참고서 reference book

사전 dictionary

10

동물원 The Zoo

저는 동물원을 좋아해요. 동물원에 가면 여러 가지 동물을 볼 수 있어요. 사자, 호랑이, 기린, 코끼리 등이 사람들한테 인기가 많아요. 어떤 동물원에서는 동물들한테 직접 먹이를 줄 수도 있어요. 그런데 너무 어린 아이들에게는 위험할 수도 있으니까 조심해야 해요.

[동무뤄늘] [조아해요]
저는 **동물원을 좋아해요**.

[동무뤄네]   [동무를] [볼 쑤] [이써요]
동물원에 가면 여러 가지 **동물을 볼 수 있어요**.

[인끼가] [마나요]
사자, 호랑이, 기린, 코끼리 등이 사람들한테* **인기가 많아요**.

[동무뤄네서는]   [직쩝] [머기를] [줄 쑤도] [이써요]
어떤 **동물원에서는** 동물들한테* **직접 먹이를 줄 수도 있어요**.

[아이드레게는]   [위험할 쑤도] [이쓰니까]
그런데 너무 어린 **아이들에게는 위험할*** 수도 있으니까 조심해야* 해요.

* 사람들한테, 동물들한테, 위험할, and 조심해야 are pronounced as 사람드란테, 동물드란테, 위허말, and 조시매야 when you say them quickly.

46

I like zoos.

You can see various animals at the zoo.

Lions, tigers, giraffes, and elephants are popular with people.

At some zoos, you can even directly feed the animals.

However it can be dangerous for children who are too young, so you have to be careful.

✎ Vocabulary   이런 단어가 나왔어요

- 동물원 zoo
- 좋아하다 to like
- 여러 가지 various, many
- 동물 animal
- 보다 to see, to watch
- 사자 lion
- 호랑이 tiger
- 기린 giraffe
- 코끼리 elephant
- 인기가 많다 to be popular
- 직접 in person

- 먹이 food, prey, fodder
- 주다 to give
- 너무 too, so, overly
- 어리다 to be young
- 아이들 kids
- 위험하다 to be dangerous
- 조심하다 to be careful

📄 Learn More   더 읽어 보세요

Animals

사자 lion	호랑이 tiger
개/강아지 dog/puppy *	고양이 cat
오리 duck	하마 hippopotamus
팬더 panda	새 bird
기린 giraffe	타조 ostrich
곰 bear	말/망아지 horse/foal *
얼룩말 zebra	코끼리 elephant
사슴 deer	소/송아지 cow/calf *
양 sheep	

* Except for puppy, foal, and calf, there are no specific words for baby animals. Instead, you can add 새끼 in front of the animal names, such as 새끼 사자, 새끼 고양이, 새끼 오리, etc.

요즘 한국에서는 캠핑이 유행이에요. 그래서 캠핑장이 많아졌어요. 캠핑장에 가면 텐트를 칠 수 있는 공간이 있어요. 그리고 캠핑장에는 화장실과 샤워실도 있어요. 전기도 사용할 수 있어요. 어떤 캠핑장에는 놀이터나 작은 수영장도 있어요. 여러 가지 체험도 할 수 있어요. 예를 들어, 땅콩도 캘 수 있고, 물고기를 잡을 수도 있어요.

* 캠핑장은 너무 덥고 심심하잖아 = Come on, it's too hot and boring at a campsite.
** 도리도리: The motion of shaking your head *** 낚시터: fishing place

49

[한구게서는]
요즘 **한국에서는** 캠핑이 유행이에요.

[마나저써요]
그래서 캠핑장이 **많아졌어요**.

[칠 쑤] [인는] [공가니] [이써요]
캠핑장에 가면 텐트를 **칠 수 있는 공간이** 있어요.

[이써요]
그리고 캠핑장에는 화장실과 샤워실도 **있어요**.

[사용할 쑤] [이써요]
전기도 **사용할 수 있어요**.

[노리터나] [자근]   . [이써요]
어떤 캠핑장에는 **놀이터나 작은** 수영장도 **있어요**.

[할 쑤] [이써요]
여러 가지 체험도 **할 수 있어요**.

[드러]   [캘 쑤] [읻꼬] [물꼬기를] [자블 쑤도] [이써요]
예를 **들어**, 땅콩도 **캘 수 있고, 물고기를 잡을 수도 있어요**.

Camping is a trend in Korea these days.

So the number of campsites has increased.

If you go to a campsite, there are places to pitch tents.

There are even bathrooms and showers at campsites.

You can even use electricity.

Some campsites also have a playground or a small swimming pool.

You can also participate in various activities.

For example, you could dig up peanuts or catch fish.

✏ Vocabulary 이런 단어가 나왔어요

- 요즘 these days
- 한국 Korea
- 캠핑 camping
- 유행 fashion, trend
- 캠핑장 camping site
- 많아지다 to increase
- 텐트 tent
- 텐트를 치다 to pitch a tent
- 공간 space, place
- 화장실 bathroom
- 샤워실 showers, shower stall
- 전기 electricity
- 사용하다 to use

- 놀이터 playground
- 작다 to be small
- 수영장 swimming pool
- 여러 가지 various
- 체험 experience, activity
- 예 example
- 땅콩 peanut
- 캐다 to dig up
- 물고기 fish
- 잡다 to catch

📄 Learn More 더 읽어 보세요

Cultural Tip

Camping is particularly popular in Korea these days so it's not difficult to find camping supply stores in most places. There are many ways to go camping in Korea, such as bringing your own tent and supplies to a 캠핑장 (campground), renting a 캠핑카 (camper car) or going 글램핑 (glamping, or 'glamourous camping' - like a hotel room in your tent!). If you don't have the time or resources for any of those, another popular way to experience camping without any of the hassle are 캠핑 카페 (camping cafés), which are cafés or restaurants where you can have barbecue and a cold drink while sitting on camping chairs inside of a pre-assembled tent.

12

아침 시간 In the Morning

저는 보통 아침 7시쯤에 일어나요. 일어나자마자 이를 닦고 샤워를 해요. 머리를 말리고 화장을 해요. 그리고 옷을 갈아입어요. 간단하게 아침을 먹어요. 주로 과일이나 떡을 먹어요. 가끔 요거트를 먹을 때도 있어요. 집에서 8시쯤에 나가요. 지하철을 타고 회사에 가요.

* 구름을 타고 출근: Going to work by riding on a cloud ** 지각이다: I'm late. *** 꿈: dream

[일곱씨쯤메][이러나요]
저는 보통 아침 **7시쯤에 일어나요.**

[이러나자마자]   [닥꼬]
일어나자마자 이를 **닦고** 샤워를 해요.

[오슬] [가라이버요]
머리를 말리고 화장을 해요. 그리고 **옷을 갈아입어요.**

[간딴하게]   [아치믈] [머거요]
간단하게* 아침을 먹어요.

[과이리나] [떠글] [머거요]
주로 **과일이나 떡을** 먹어요.

[머글]   [이써요]
가끔 요거트를 **먹을** 때도 **있어요.**

[지베서][여덜씨쯤메]
집에서 8시쯤에 나가요.

[지하처를]
지하철을 타고 회사에 가요.

* 간단하게 is pronounced as 간따나게 when you say it quickly.

54

I usually wake up around 7 in the morning.

As soon as I wake up, I brush my teeth and take a shower.

I dry my hair and do my makeup. Then I change my clothes.

I have a simple breakfast.

I usually eat fruit or rice cakes.

Sometimes I eat yogurt.

I leave the house at about 8 o'clock.

I ride the subway and go to work.

✏ Vocabulary 이런 단어가 나왔어요

- 보통 usually
- 아침 morning
- 일어나다 to wake up
- 이를 닦다 to brush one's teeth
- 샤워하다 to take a shower
- 머리 hair
- 말리다 to dry
- 화장 makeup
- 옷 clothes
- 갈아 입다 to change one's clothes
- 간단하다 to be simple
- 먹다 to eat
- 주로 mainly, mostly
- 과일 fruit

- 떡 rice cake
- 가끔 sometimes
- 요거트 yogurt
- 집 house
- 나가다 to go out
- 지하철 subway
- 타다 to ride
- 회사 work, company
- 가다 to go

📄 Learn More 더 읽어 보세요

Expressions Related to Daily Life

일어나다 to wake up
먹다 to eat
일하다 to work
통화하다 to talk on the phone
출근하다 to go to work
퇴근하다 to go home from work
학교에 가다 to go to school
집에 가다 to go home
자다 to sleep

샤워하다 to take a shower
만나다 to meet
공부하다 to study

13

택배 Deliveries

요즘에는 모든 물건을 인터넷으로 살 수 있어요. 한국에서는 인터넷으로 물건을 주문하면 보통 2~3일 안에 물건을 받을 수 있어요. 어떤 쇼핑몰에서는 오늘 주문하면 내일 택배를 받을 수 있어요. 또 어떤 곳에서는 오후 2시 전에 주문하면 그날 저녁에 받을 수 있어요. 옷이나 책뿐만 아니라 과일이나 달걀까지 인터넷으로 주문할 수 있어요.

* 이제 좀 쉴까: Shall I rest now? ** 띵동: The sound of a doorbell *** 당일배송: Same day delivery

[요즈메는] [물거늘] [인터네스로] [살 쑤] [이써요]
요즘에는 모든 **물건을 인터넷으로 살 수 있어요.**

[한구게서는] [인터네스로] [물거늘] [이사밀] [아네] [물거늘]
한국에서는 인터넷으로 물건을 주문하면* 보통 **2~3일** 안에 **물건을**
[바들 쑤] [이써요]
받을 수 있어요.

[쇼핑모레서는] [택빠를] [바들 쑤] [이써요]
어떤 **쇼핑몰에서는** 오늘 주문하면* 내일 **택배를 받을 수 있어요.**

[고세서는] [두시] [저네] [저녀게] [바들 쑤]
또 어떤 **곳에서는** 오후 **2시 전에** 주문하면* 그날 **저녁에 받을 수**
[이써요]
있어요.

[오시나] [과이리나] [인터네스로] [주문할 쑤]
옷이나 책뿐만 아니라 **과일이나** 달걀까지 **인터넷으로 주문할* 수**
[이써요]
있어요.

* 주문하면 and 주문할 are pronounced as 주무나면 and 주무날 when you say them quickly.

These days, you can buy everything on the Internet.

In Korea, when you order something on the Internet, you can usually get it within 2-3 days.

For some online shopping malls, if you order today, you can receive the delivery tomorrow.

For some places, if you order before 2pm, you can get it that evening.

You can order not only clothes or books, but you can even order fruit or eggs online.

✎ Vocabulary 이런 단어가 나왔어요

- 요즘 these days
- 모든 every
- 물건 thing, stuff, goods
- 인터넷 Internet
- 사다 to buy
- 주문하다 to order
- 보통 usually
- 안 within, inside
- 받다 to receive
- 오늘 today

- 내일 tomorrow
- 택배 parcel delivery service
- 곳 place
- 오후 afternoon
- 전 before
- 그날 that day
- 옷 clothes
- 책 book
- 과일 fruit
- 달걀 egg

📄 Learn More 더 읽어 보세요

Cultural Tip

Internet shopping is extremely convenient in Korea. Many online shopping malls have expedited shipping services that allow you to purchase a product and receive it within 24 hours or less! These shopping malls also typically allow you to set all of your delivery preferences so that the 택배원/택배기사 (delivery person) knows exactly what to do with your package. When you purchase something, you can enter your preferences along with your mobile phone number at checkout, then once the delivery arrives, the delivery person will either text you or call you, depending on your preference, to let you know it has arrived. Some services will even take a photo of your package and send it to you so you can rest assured that everything was handled properly!

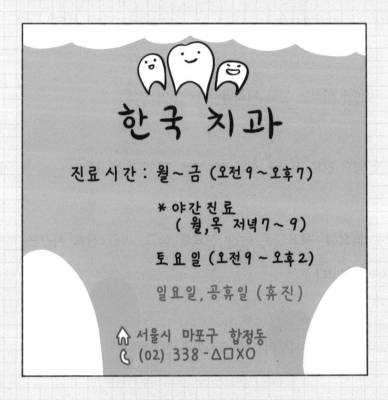

한국 치과

진료 시간 : 월~금 (오전 9 ~ 오후 7)

* 야간 진료
(월, 목 저녁 7 ~ 9)

토 요 일 (오전 9 ~ 오후 2)

일요일, 공휴일 (휴진)

서울시 마포구 합정동
(02) 338 - △□XO

전화 주셔서 감사합니다. 늘 정성을 다하는 한국 치과입니다. 저희 병원 진료 시간은 평일 9시부터 7시까지입니다. 매주 월요일, 목요일은 야간 진료를 하고, 야간 진료 시간은 저녁 9시까지입니다. 토요일은 오전 9시부터 오후 2시까지 진료합니다. 일요일, 공휴일은 휴진입니다. 감사합니다.

[감사합니다]
전화* 주셔서 **감사합니다.**

[치꽈임니다]
늘 정성을 다하는 한국 **치과입니다.**

[저히]　　[질료] [시가는]　　[아홉씨부터][일곱씨까지임니다]
저희 병원 **진료 시간**은 평일 **9시부터 7시까지입니다.**

[워료일]　[모교이른]　　[질료를]　　　[질료] [시가는]
매주 **월요일, 목요일**은 야간 **진료를** 하고, 야간 **진료 시간**은 저녁
[아홉씨까지임니다]
9시까지입니다.

[토요이른]　　[아홉씨부터]　　[두시까지] [질료함니다]
토요일은 오전 **9시부터** 오후 **2시까지 진료합니다.**

[이료일]　[공휴이른]　[휴지님니다]
일요일, 공휴일은 **휴진입니다.**

[감사합니다]
감사합니다.

* 전화 is pronounced as 저놔 when you say it quickly.

Thank you for calling.

We are Korean Dental Clinic and we always do our best.

Our clinical hours are from 9 to 7 on weekdays.

We provide evening treatment services every Monday and Thursday until 9pm.

On Saturdays, we are open from 9am to 2pm.

On Sundays and public holidays, we are closed.

Thank you.

✐ Vocabulary 이런 단어가 나왔어요

- 전화 telephone
- 감사하다 to appreciate, to thank
- 정성을 다하다 to put your heart into, to do one's best
- 치과 dental clinic
- 병원 hospital
- 진료 시간 consultation hours, clinical hours
- 평일 weekday
- 매주 every week
- 월요일 Monday
- 목요일 Thursday
- 야간 night, night time, evening

- 진료 medical treatment
- 시간 time
- 오전 in the morning, am
- 오후 in the evening, pm
- 일요일 Sunday
- 공휴일 public holiday
- 휴진 non-consultation day

📄 Learn More 더 읽어 보세요

Phrases You Hear During a Phone Consultation

안녕하십니까. Hello.

사랑합니다. 고객님. I appreciate you, Customer.

정성을 다하는 OO입니다. I'm the meticulous OO.

무엇을 도와 드릴까요? How can I help you?

상담원 OOO였습니다. This has been the consultant, OOO.

오늘도 좋은 하루 보내십시오. Have a nice day.

15

회식 Company Dinners

저희 회사는 회식을 자주 해요. 어제도 회식을 했어요. 어제는 저희 팀 사람들끼리만 회식을 했어요. 일 년에 한 번 정도, 전체 회식을 해요. 그때는 회사의 모든 사람들이 모여서 회식을 해요. 팀 사람들끼리는 자주 회식을 해요. 주로 저녁을 먹으면서 간단하게 술을 마셔요. 가끔 술을 아주 많이 마실 때도 있어요.

* 공지사항: announcement ** 금일: today *** 장소: place

[저히]　　　[회시글]
저희 회사는 **회식을** 자주 해요.

[회시글] [헤써요]
어제도 **회식을** **했어요.**

[저히]　　　　　　[회시글] [해써요]
어제는 **저희** 팀 사람들끼리만 **회식을** **했어요.**

[녀네]　　　　　　　　[회시글]
일 **년에** 한 번 정도, 전체 **회식을** 해요.

[회사의 or 회사에]　[사람드리]　　　[회시글]
그때는 **회사의** 모든 **사람들이** 모여서 **회식을** 해요.

[회시글]
팀 사람들끼리는 자주 **회식을** 해요.

[저녀글] [머그면서] [간딴하게]　[수를]
주로 **저녁을 먹으면서 간단하게*** **술을** 마셔요.

[수를]　　[마니]　　　[이써요]
가끔 **술을** 아주 **많이** 마실 때도 **있어요.**

* 간단하게 is pronounced as 간따나게 when you say it quickly.

Our workplace often has company dinners.

We had a company dinner yesterday, too.

Yesterday, only our team members had dinner together.

We have a company-wide dinner about once a year.

At that time, everyone in the company gathers for dinner.

Within our team, we often have dinners.

We usually have a light drink while having dinner.

Sometimes there are times when we drink a lot, too.

✏ Vocabulary 이런 단어가 나왔어요

- 회사 workplace, company
- 회식 company dinner
- 자주 often
- 어제 yesterday
- 사람들 people
- -끼리 privately, among ourselves
- 일 년 one year
- 정도 about, around
- 전체 whole
- 모든 every
- 모이다 to gather
- 저녁 dinner

- 먹다 to eat
- 간단하다 to be simple
- 술을 마시다 to drink
- 아주 very
- 많이 a lot, many, much

📄 Learn More 더 읽어 보세요

Cultural Tip

Company dinners are common in the majority of Korean workplaces. Although not mandatory, it is still frowned upon to miss the dinners as they are seen as a team-building activity meant to bring employees closer. A popular spot for company dinners are barbecue restaurants, where juniors will pour drinks and grill meat for their seniors as a sign of respect. After eating, the group will often move to 2차 (second spot or second round) and maybe even 3차 (3rd spot or 3rd round), with bars and karaoke rooms being common places.

16

생일 Birthdays

오늘은 생일이니까 미역국을 끓여 줘야지

미역 (Sea Weed)
- 피를 맑게 해 주고
상처를 낫게 해 준다

다 됐다~

이게 뭐야!

미역 말고 생선 줘!!

생일 축하해

한국에서는 생일에 미역국을 먹어요. 미역은 피를 맑게 해 주고, 상처를 낫게 해 줘요. 그래서 옛날부터 엄마들은 아기를 낳은 후에 미역국을 먹었어요. 그러면 생일에는 왜 미역국을 먹을까요? 엄마가 나를 힘들게 낳아 줬잖아요. 그래서 자신이 태어난 생일에, 낳아 준 엄마에게 감사하는 마음에서 먹기 시작했다고 해요.

* 오늘 생일이니까 미역국을 끓여 줘야지: Since it's his/her birthday today, I'll make seaweed soup for him/her. ** 다 됐다: It's done! *** 미역 말고 생선 줘: Give me fish, not seaweed.

69

[한구게서는] [생이레] [미역꾸글] [머거요]
한국에서는 생일에 **미역국을 먹어요.**

[미여근] [말께] [낟께]
미역은 피를 맑게 해 주고, 상처를 **낫게** 해 줘요.

[옌날부터] [엄마드른] [나은] [미역꾸글] [머거써요]
그래서 **옛날부터 엄마들은** 아기를 **낳은** 후에 **미역국을 먹었어요.**

[생이레는] [미역꾸글] [머글까요]
그러면 **생일에는** 왜 **미역국을 먹을까요?**

[나아] [줟짜나요]
엄마가 나를 힘들게 **낳아 줬잖아요.**

[자시니] [생이레] [나아] [마으메서]
그래서 **자신이** 태어난 **생일에, 낳아** 준 엄마에게 감사하는 **마음에서**
[먹끼] [시자캗따고]
먹기 시작했다고 해요.

Translation 이런 뜻이에요

In Korea, we eat seaweed soup on our birthday.

Seaweed cleanses the blood and heals wounds.

Because of this, mothers have long eaten seaweed soup after giving birth to a baby.

Then why do we eat seaweed on our birthday?

Our moms went through a hard time to give birth to us.

It is said that we started to eat seaweed soup to show thanks to our mothers on our birthday.

✐ Vocabulary 이런 단어가 나왔어요

- 생일 birthday
- 미역국 seaweed soup
- 먹다 to eat
- 피 blood
- 맑다 to be clear, to be clean
- 상처 wound
- 낫다 to be healed
- 옛날 old days, past
- 엄마 mom
- 아기 baby
- 낳다 to give birth to
- 후 after

- 왜 why
- 힘들다 to be hard, to be tough
- 태어나다 to be born
- 감사하다 to thank, to appreciate
- 마음 heart, mind
- 시작하다 to start

📄 Learn More 더 읽어 보세요

Expressions Related to Birthdays

생일 축하해요. Happy Birthday!

생일 선물 birthday present

생일 케이크 birthday cake

생일 카드 birthday card

생일 파티 birthday party

깜짝 파티 surprise party

생일 축하 노래 birthday song

생일 소원 birthday wish

소원을 빌다 to make a wish

케이크를 자르다 to cut the cake

초를 불다 to blow out the candles

17

안내방송 Announcements

동물원에 오신 것을 환영합니다. 저희 동물원에서는 동물 먹이 주기 행사를 하고 있습니다. 10시에는 돌고래에게 먹이 주는 모습을 보실 수 있습니다. 12시에는 귀여운 앵무새에게 먹이를 직접 주는 행사가 있습니다. 어린이 동물원에서는 아기 동물들에게 수시로 먹이를 주실 수 있습니다. 한 달 전에 태어난 아기 백호랑이도 만나 보실 수 있습니다. 저희 동물원에서 즐거운 추억 많이 남기시길 바라겠습니다.

[동무뤄네]　　　[거슬] [화녕함니다]
동물원에 오신 것을 환영합니다.

[저히] [동무뤄네서는]　　　[머기]　　　　　　[이씀니다]
저희 동물원에서는 동물 먹이 주기 행사를 하고 있습니다.

[열씨에는]　　　　　[머기]　　[모스블] [보실 쑤] [읻씀니다]
10시에는 돌고래에게 먹이 주는 모습을 보실 수 있습니다.

[열뚜시에는]　　　　　　　　　[머기를] [직쩝]　　　　　[읻씀니다]
12시에는 귀여운 앵무새에게 먹이를 직접 주는 행사가 있습니다.

[어리니]　[동무뤄네서는]　　　　[동물드레게]　　　[머기를]　[주실 쑤]
어린이 동물원에서는 아기 동물들에게 수시로 먹이를 주실 수
[읻씀니다]
있습니다.

　　　　[저네]　　　　　　[배코랑이도]　　　[보실 쑤] [읻씀니다]
한 달 전에 태어난 아기 백호랑이도 만나 보실 수 있습니다.

　　　[동무뤄네서]　　　　　　[마니]　　　[바라겓씀니다]
저희 동물원에서 즐거운 추억 많이 남기시길 바라겠습니다.

Welcome to the zoo.

At our zoo, we are having an event for feeding the animals.

At 10 o'clock, you can see the dolphins being fed.

At 12 o'clock, there is an event where you can feed the cute parrots yourself.

At the children's zoo, you can feed the baby animals at any time.

You can also meet baby white tigers that were born a month ago.

We hope you will make lots of fun memories at our zoo.

✎ Vocabulary 이런 단어가 나왔어요

- 동물원 zoo
- 환영하다 to welcome
- 먹이 food, prey, fodder
- 모습 how one looks, how a certain place or a thing looks
- 행사 event
- 돌고래 dolphin
- 보다 to see, to watch
- 귀엽다 to be cute
- 앵무새 parrot
- 직접 in person

- 아기 baby
- 수시로 frequently, often
- 한 달 one month
- 태어나다 to be born
- 백호랑이 white tiger
- 만나 보다 to meet
- 즐겁다 to be pleasant, to be pleased, to be enjoyable
- 추억 memory
- 남기다 to leave
- 바라다 to hope

📄 Learn More 더 읽어 보세요

Cultural Tip

There are two words for 'event' in Korean: 행사 and 이벤트. 행사 is used for an event of any kind, such as the "animal feeding event" seen in this passage. However, if you ever see the second one(이벤트) it is referring to not just any event, but a sale of some sort. For example, during the Harvest Festival in Korea, you may see banners displayed in many stores with "추석 이벤트! 30% 할인!" stating that they're having a 30% off sale for the holidays. There is one other situation where you might see 이벤트 if you're particularly romantic. 백일 이벤트! The "100 days event" is something many couples do when they have been together for 100 days. For example, one person will surprise their partner with a romantic set-up of balloons, flowers, and votive candles arranged in a heart shape. Just be careful if you ever try to plan a 백일 이벤트 yourself, as all those votives can be a fire hazard!

18

초대 Invitation

안녕하세요, 지나인의 최경은입니다. 저희 회사가 만들어진 지 벌써 10년이 되었습니다. 그동안 도움 주신 모든 분들께 감사드립니다. 10주년을 맞이해서 작은 행사를 준비했습니다. 간단한 식사 및 이벤트가 있을 예정입니다. 행사는 2019년 9월 1일 저녁 6시부터 진행됩니다. 많은 참석 부탁드립니다.

---

* 축하 이벤트: Celebratory event ** 방탄소년단: K-Pop boy band, BTS *** 방탄소년단 노래와 춤을 저희가 해 보겠습니다: We will sing and dance to a BTS song by ourselves.

Read Out Loud and Practice Pronunciation 큰 소리로 읽어 보세요

[최경으님니다]
안녕하세요, **지나인의 최경은입니다.**
[지나이늬 or 지나이네]

[저히]   [만드러진]   [심녀니] [되얻씀니다]
저희 회사가 **만들어진** 지 벌써 **10년이 되었습니다.**

[감사드림니다]
그동안 도움 주신 모든 분들께 **감사드립니다.**

[십쭈녀늘] [마지해서] [자근]   [준비핻씀니다]
10주년을 맞이해서 작은 행사를 **준비했습니다.**

[간딴한] [식싸] [믿]   [이쓸] [예정임니다]
간단한* 식사 및 이벤트가 있을 **예정입니다.**

          [이천십꾸년][구월][이릴]   [여섣씨부터] [진행됨니다]
행사는 **2019년 9월 1일** 저녁 **6시부터 진행됩니다*.**

[마는]   [부탁드림니다]
많은 참석 **부탁드립니다.**

* 간단한 and 진행됩니다 are pronounced as 간따난 and 지냉됨니다 when you say them quickly.

78

Hello, I'm Kyeong-eun Choi of G9.

It has already been 10 years since our company was created.

Thank you all for your help until now.

To celebrate our 10th anniversary, we have prepared a small event.

There will be a simple meal and an event.

The event will be held at 6pm on September 1st, 2019.

We look forward to your attendance.

✐ Vocabulary   이런 단어가 나왔어요

- 회사 company
- 만들어지다 to be made
- 벌써 already
- 그동안 meanwhile, meantime
- 도움 help
- 주다 to give
- 모든 every
- 분 numerical counter for people
- 감사드리다 to thank, to appreciate
- 맞이하다 to celebrate, to meet
- 작다 to be small
- 행사 event
- 준비하다 to prepare
- 간단하다 to be simple
- 식사 meal
- 이벤트 event
- 예정 schedule
- 저녁 dinner
- 진행되다 to go along
- 참석 attendance
- 부탁 드리다 to ask, to request

📄 Learn More   더 읽어 보세요

Expressions Related to E-mail

받은 편지함 inbox	보낸 편지함 sent mail
스팸 메일 spam mail	보내기 send
전송 send	답장 reply
전체 답장 reply to all	회신 reply
전달 forwarding	참조 reference
읽음 read	삭제 delete
첨부 attachment	

한국에서는 요즘 1일 1팩이 유행이에요. 매일 팩을 하나씩 하면 피부가 좋아진다고 해요. 특히 공기가 건조한 겨울에는 보습이 중요해요. 요즘에는 마스크 팩이 다양한 종류로 나와요. 캐릭터가 그려진 마스크 팩도 있어요. 천연 재료를 사용한 마스크 팩도 인기가 많아요. 꿀이나 오이처럼 천연 재료를 이용한 마스크 팩이에요.

* 어흥: roar ** 살려 주세요: Please save me. *** 훌쩍: The sound or motion of sniffling while crying

81

[한구게서는]　　[이릴][일패기]
한국에서는 요즘 **1일 1팩이** 유행이에요.

[패글]　[하나씨 카면]　　　　[조아진다고]
매일 **팩을 하나씩 하면** 피부가 **좋아진다고** 해요.

[트키]　　　　　　[겨우레는] [보스비]
특히 공기가 건조한 **겨울에는 보습이** 중요해요.

[요즈메는]　　　[패기]　　　[종뉴로]
요즘에는 마스크 **팩이** 다양한 **종류로** 나와요.

[팩또] [이써요]
캐릭터가 그려진 마스크 **팩도 있어요.**

[처년]　　　　　　　　[팩또] [인끼가] [마나요]
천연 재료를 사용한 마스크 **팩도 인기가 많아요.**

[꾸리나]　　　　[처년]　　　　　　[패기에요]
꿀이나 오이처럼 **천연** 재료를 이용한 마스크 **팩이에요.**

In Korea, these days "one mask pack a day" is trending.

If you use one facial mask pack every day, they say your skin will improve.

Moisturization is especially important in winter when the air is dry.

These days, mask packs come in various kinds.

There are also mask packs with characters drawn on them.

Mask packs using natural materials are also popular.

These mask packs use natural ingredients like honey or cucumber.

- 요즘 these days
- 유행 fashion, trend
- 매일 every day
- 팩 mask
- 하나씩 one piece each
- 피부 skin
- 좋아지다 to improve, to become better
- 특히 especially
- 공기 air
- 건조하다 to be dry
- 겨울 winter
- 보습 moisturization

- 중요하다 to be important
- 다양하다 to be varied
- 종류 kind, sort
- 나오다 to come out, to appear, to be released
- 그려지다 to be drawn
- 천연 natural
- 재료 material
- 사용하다 to use
- 인기가 많다 to be popular
- 꿀 honey
- 오이 cucumber
- 이용하다 to use

📄 Learn More   더 읽어 보세요

Types of Cosmetics

화장품 cosmetic products

화장하다 to make up, to put on makeup

스킨 toner

선크림 sunblock

파운데이션 foundation

아이라이너 eyeliner

마스카라 mascara

블러셔/볼터치 blush

로션 lotion

베이스 base

아이브로우 eyebrow makeup

아이섀도우 eyeshadow

립스틱 lipstick

속눈썹 eyelashes

20

편지 Letters

주석이에게.

주석아, 오랜만이야. 잘 지내지? 그 곳은 어때? 한국은 점점 추워지고 있어. 벌써 겨울이 온 것 같아. 거기는 따뜻해서 좋겠다. 우리 겨울 되면 항상 눈사람 만들었잖아. 기억나? 이번 겨울에는 한국에 올 거지? 나요즘 요리 연습하고 있어. 한국에 오면 맛있는 것 많이 만들어 줄게. 그럼 그때까지 잘 지내. 보고 싶어.

2018년 10월 30일. 경은이가.

* 우리 선생님 닮았다: It looks like our teacher.

[주서기에게]
주석이에게.

[주서가] [오랜마니야]
주석아, 오랜만이야. 잘 지내지?

[고슨] [한구근] [이써]
그 **곳은** 어때? **한국은** 점점 추워지고 **있어.**

[겨우리] [가타] [따뜨태서] [조켇따]
벌써 **겨울이** 온 것 **같아.** 거기는 **따뜻해서 좋겠다.**

[눈싸람] [만드런짜나] [기엉나]
우리 겨울 되면 항상 **눈사람 만들었잖아. 기억나?**

[겨우레는] [한구게] [올 꺼지] [연스파고] [이써]
이번 **겨울에는 한국에 올 거지?** 나 요즘 요리 **연습하고 있어.**

[한구게] [마신는] [걷] [마니] [만드러] [줄께]
한국에 오면 **맛있는 것 많이 만들어 줄게.**

[시퍼]
그럼 그때까지 잘 지내. 보고 **싶어.**

[이천십팔련][시월] [삼시빌] [경으니가]
2018년 10월 30일. 경은이가.

Dear Joo-seok,

Joo-seok, it's been a while. How are you?

What is it like over there? Korea is getting colder.

It feels like it's already winter. It's warm there so it must be nice.

We always made snowmen in the winter, you know. Do you remember?

You're coming to Korea this winter, right? I'm practicing cooking these days.

I will make a lot of delicious things for you when you come to Korea.

Well, until then, take care. I miss you.

October 30th, 2018. Kyeong-eun.

✎ Vocabulary   이런 단어가 나왔어요

- 오랜만이다 to have been a while
- 곳 place
- 점점 more and more
- 추워지다 to become colder
- 벌써 already
- 겨울 winter
- 오다 to come
- 거기 there
- 따뜻하다 to be warm
- 좋다 to be good
- 항상 always
- 눈사람 snowman
- 만들다 to make

- 기억나다 to remember
- 이번 this
- 요즘 these days
- 요리 cooking
- 연습하다 to practice
- 오다 to come
- 맛있다 to be delicious
- 많이 a lot, many, much
- 만들어 주다 to make something for someone
- 보고 싶다 to miss

📄 Learn More   더 읽어 보세요

Common Ways to Say "How have you been?" in a Letter

잘 지내지? You're doing well, right? (casual)

잘 지냈어? Have you been well? (casual)

잘 지내고 있어? Are you doing well? (casual)

잘 지내죠? You're doing well, right? (formal)

잘 지내시죠? You're doing well, right? (formal, honorific)

그동안 어떻게 지냈어? How have you been? (casual)

그동안 어떻게 지내셨어요? How have you been? (formal, honorific)

21

가을 Autumn

한국은 가을에 여행하기 정말 좋아요. 한국에는 산이 정말 많아요. 가을이 되면 모든 산이 빨간색, 노란색으로 변해요. 10월 초가 되면 단풍이 들기 시작해요. 그때쯤에 강원도에 있는 산에 가면 좋아요. 10월 말이 되면 서울에도 단풍이 들기 시작해요.

* 산이 너무 멋지다!: The mountains look awesome! ** 역시 가을 여행이 최고: Indeed, traveling in autumn is the best. *** 찰칵: The sound of clicking the shutter (taking a photo)

[한구근] [가으레]   [조아요]
한국은 가을에 여행하기 정말 **좋아요.**

[한구게는] [사니]   [마나요]
한국에는 산이 정말 **많아요.**

[가으리]   [사니]   [노란새그로]
가을이 되면 모든 **산이** 빨간색, **노란색으로** 변해요*.

[시월]   [시자캐요]
10월 초가 되면 단풍이 들기 **시작해요.**

[그때쯔메]   [인는] [사네]   [조아요]
그때쯤에 강원도에 **있는 산에** 가면 **좋아요.**

[시월] [마리]   [서우레도]   [시자캐요]
10월 말이 되면 **서울에도** 단풍이 들기 **시작해요.**

* 변해요 is pronounced as 벼내요 when you say it quickly.

Korea is very good for traveling in autumn.

There are a lot of mountains in Korea.

In autumn, all the mountains turn red and yellow.

At the beginning of October, the leaves begin to change colors.

It is nice to go to the mountains in Gangwon-do around that time.

By the end of October, the leaves begin to change colors in Seoul, too.

✐ Vocabulary   이런 단어가 나왔어요

- 가을 autumn, fall
- 여행하다 to travel
- 좋다 to be good
- 산 mountain
- 정말 really
- 많다 to be a lot
- 모든 every
- 빨간색 red
- 노란색 yellow
- 변하다 to be changed
- 초 beginning of
- 단풍 fall foliage

- (단풍이) 들다 to turn (red/yellow)
- 시작하다 to start
- 그때쯤 about that time, around then
- 말 end of

📄 Learn More   더 읽어 보세요

Cultural Tip

With so many mountains, one of Korea's most popular pastimes is hiking. There are many subway stations located next to these mountains; particularly in the more tepid months during spring and autumn, people decked out from head to toe in hiking gear can often be seen riding the subway to these spots on their way to a group hike. Hiking is especially popular among middle-aged people as a social activity, and they will often pack their backpacks with snacks and instant coffee to share once they've reached the summit. Hiking is so popular that it is not difficult to find a brand selling exclusively hiking supplies and clothing, and even major big-box stores often have a hiking section.

22

치매 Dementia

치매는 뇌의 신경 세포가 손상되는 병이에요. 치매에 걸리면 기억을 잘 못 해요. 그리고 의지와 상관없이 행동을 하게 돼요. 주로 노인들에게 생기는 병이에요. 그렇지만 요즘에는 젊은 사람들도 치매에 많이 걸린 다고 해요. 치매 예방에 좋은 음식을 소개할게요. 블루베리, 굴, 시금 치, 올리브 오일, 연어 등이 좋다고 해요. 꾸준히 운동을 하는 것도 도움 이 되겠죠?

[뇌의 or 뇌에]
치매는 **뇌의** 신경 세포가 손상되는 병이에요.

[기어글]　　[모 태요]
치매에 걸리면 **기억을** 잘 **못 해요.**

[상과넙씨]
그리고 의지와 **상관없이** 행동을 하게 돼요.

[노인드레게]
주로 **노인들에게** 생기는 병이에요.

[그러치만] [요즈메는] [절믄]　　　　　[마니]
그렇지만 요즘에는 젊은 사람들도 치매에 **많이** 걸린다고 해요.

[조은] [음시글] [소개할께요]
치매 예방에 **좋은 음식을 소개할게요.**

[여너]　　[조타고]
블루베리, 굴, 시금치, 올리브 오일, **연어** 등이 **좋다고** 해요.

[걷또] [도우미]
꾸준히* 운동을 하는 **것도 도움이** 되겠죠?

---

* 꾸준히 is pronounced as 꾸주니 when you say it quickly.

Dementia is a disease that damages the brain's nerve cells.

If you have dementia, you can't remember things well.

You also act regardless of your volition.

It's mainly a disease appearing in the elderly.

However nowadays, they say many young people are also developing dementia.

I'll introduce some good foods to help prevent dementia.

They say blueberries, oysters, spinach, olive oil, and salmon are good.

It would probably be helpful to exercise consistently too, wouldn't it?

✐ Vocabulary   이런 단어가 나왔어요

- 치매 dementia
- 뇌 brain
- 신경 nerve
- 세포 cell
- 손상되다 to be damaged
- 병 disease
- (병에) 걸리다 to get sick
- 기억 memory
- 의지 volition
- 상관없다 to have nothing to do with
- 행동 action
- 주로 mainly, mostly
- 노인 elderly
- 요즘 these days

- 젊다 to be young
- 사람들 people
- 예방 prevention
- 좋다 to be good
- 음식 food
- 소개하다 introduce
- 블루베리 blueberry
- 굴 oyster
- 시금치 spinach
- 올리브 오일 olive oil
- 연어 salmon
- 꾸준히 consistently, constantly
- 운동 exercise
- 도움이 되다 to be helpful

🗒 Learn More   더 읽어 보세요

Expressions Related to Diseases

병 disease, illness
병을 얻다 to get a disease
진료 받다 to consult a doctor
처방전을 받다 to receive a prescription
약을 먹다 to take medicine
주사를 맞다 to have an injection
수술하다 to operate, to get an operation
병이 낫다 to get well, to be cured

병에 걸리다 to get sick, to fall ill
병원에 가다 to go to the hospital
치료 받다 to be treated

23

취미 Hobbies

저는 등산을 좋아해요. 주로 혼자 등산을 해요. 등산을 시작한 지 5년 정도 되었어요. 처음에는 친구들과 함께 등산을 했어요. 그런데 요즘에는 혼자 등산을 하는 게 좋아요. 처음에는 산 정상에 올라가는 게 정말 힘들었어요. 이제는 산 정상까지 쉽게 올라갈 수 있어요.

* 언제부터: from when

[등사늘] [조아해요]
저는 **등산을 좋아해요.**

[등사늘]
주로 혼자 **등산을** 해요.

[등사늘] [시자칸]   [오년]   [되어써요]
등산을 시작한 지 **5년** 정도 **되었어요.**

[처으메는]   [등사늘] [해써요]
처음에는 친구들과 함께 **등산을 했어요.**

[요즈메는]   [등사늘]   [조아요]
그런데 **요즘에는** 혼자 **등산을** 하는 게 **좋아요.**

[처으메는]   [힘드러써요]
처음에는 산 정상에 올라가는 게 정말 **힘들었어요.**

[쉽께] [올라갈 쑤] [이써요]
이제는 산 정상까지 **쉽게 올라갈 수 있어요.**

I like hiking.

For the most part, I hike alone.

It has been about 5 years since I started hiking.

At first, I hiked with my friends.

However nowadays, I like to hike alone.

At first it was really hard to get to the top of the mountain.

Now I can easily go up to the top.

✎ Vocabulary 이런 단어가 나왔어요

- 등산 climbing
- 좋아하다 to like
- 주로 mostly, mainly
- 혼자 alone
- 시작하다 to start
- 정도 about, around
- 처음 first
- 친구들과 with friends
- 함께 together
- 요즘 these days
- 정상 top
- 올라가다 to go up
- 정말 really

- 힘들다 to be hard, to be tough
- 이제 now
- 쉽다 to be easy

📄 Learn More 더 읽어 보세요

Talking About for How Long You've Been Doing Something

When discussing hobbies, people will often ask how long you have been doing a particular hobby or when you started. You might reply, "I've been doing ~ for about [time]" which in Korean is "~한 지 [시간] 정도 되었다". To put it more simply, "It has been about [time] since I began." which is "시작한 지 [시간] 정도 되었다". For example, if your hobby is programming and you have been doing it for about 3 years, you could say "프로그래밍을 한 지 3년 정도 되었어요" or simply, "시작한 지 3년 정도 되었어요".

24

소개 Introductions

제 친구를 한 명 소개할게요. 이름은 최수지예요. 저랑 초등학교 때부터 친구예요. 저랑 가장 친한 친구예요. 수지는 성격이 밝아요. 그리고 사람 만나는 걸 정말 좋아해요. 그래서 주변에 아는 사람들이 많아요. 수지 덕분에 저도 새로운 친구를 많이 사귀었어요.

* 스페인에서 만난 카를로스야: This is Carlos who I met in Spain. ** 일본에서 만난 오카모토 군 기타리스트야: This is Okamoto who I met in Japan. He's a guitarist. *** 호호호, 하하: The sound or motion of laughing

[소개할께요]
제 친구를 한 명 **소개할게요**.

[이르믄]
이름은 최수지예요.

[초등학꾜]
저랑 **초등학교** 때부터 친구예요.

저랑 가장 친한* 친구예요.

[성껴기] [발가요]
수지는 **성격이 밝아요**.

[조아해요]
그리고 사람 만나는 걸 정말 **좋아해요**.

[주벼네] [사람드리] [마나요]
그래서 **주변에** 아는 **사람들이 많아요**.

[덕뿌네] [마니] [사귀어써요]
수지 **덕분에** 저도 새로운 친구를 **많이 사귀었어요**.

* 친한 is pronounced as 치난 when you say it quickly.

I'll introduce a friend of mine.

Her name is Soo-ji Choi.

I have been friends with her since elementary school.

She's my best friend.

Soo-ji has a bright personality.

She really loves meeting people.

So she knows a lot of people around her.

Thanks to Soo-ji, I have also made lots of new friends.

✏ Vocabulary 이런 단어가 나왔어요

- 친구 friend
- 명 numerical counter for people
- 소개하다 to introduce
- 초등학교 elementary school
- 가장 the most
- 친하다 to be close
- 성격 character, personality
- 밝다 to be bright, to be cheerful
- 사람 person
- 만나다 to meet
- 좋아하다 to like
- 주변에 around
- 알다 to know

- 덕분에 thanks to
- 새롭다 to be new
- 사귀다 to get along

📄 Learn More 더 읽어 보세요

Types of Personalities

성격이 밝아요. He/She is bright/sunny.

성격이 좋아요. He/She has a nice personality.

성격이 차분해요. He/She has a calm personality.

성격이 내성적이에요. He/She is introverted.

성격이 외향적이에요. He/She is extroverted.

성격이 소심해요. He/She is a timid person.

성격이 활발해요. He/She is outgoing.

성격이 조용해요. He/She is quiet.

25

반려동물 Pets

동물을 키우는 사람들이 점점 늘어나고 있어요. 예전에는 사람들과 함께 생활하는 동물을 '애완동물'이라고 불렀어요. 사람에게 즐거움을 주기 위한 동물이라는 뜻이에요. 그런데 요즘에는 '반려동물'이라고 부르는 사람들이 많아졌어요. 친구나 가족과 같은 존재라는 뜻이에요. 반려동물로 보통 개와 고양이를 많이 키워요.

---

* 아하, 우리 실버를 말하는구나: Oh, I see that it refers to my dear Silver.

[동무를]　　　　　[사람드리]　　　[느러나고] [이써요]
동물을 키우는 **사람들이** 점점 **늘어나고** 있어요.

[예저네는]　　　　　　　　　　　　　　　　　[동무를] [애완동무리라고]　　[불러써요]
예전에는 사람들과 함께 생활하는* **동물을 '애완동물'이라고** 불렀어요.

[사라메게]　[즐거우믈]　　　　　　　[동무리라는]　[뜨시에요]
사람에게 즐거움을 주기 위한 **동물이라는 뜻이에요.**

　　　　[요즈메는]　　[발려동무리라고]　　　　　　[사람드리] [마나저써요]
그런데 **요즘에는 '반려동물'이라고** 부르는 **사람들이 많아졌어요.**

　　　　　　[가족꽈] [가튼]　　　　　[뜨시에요]
친구나 **가족과 같은** 존재라는 **뜻이에요.**

[발려동물로]　　　　　　　　　　　[마니]
반려동물로 보통 개와 고양이를 **많이** 키워요.

---

* 생활하는 is pronounced as 생화라는 when you say it quickly.

More and more people are raising animals.

In the past, animals that lived with people were called "pets".

It meant animals whose purpose was to bring people joy.

However nowadays, there are many people who call them "companion animals".

This phrase means being more like a friend or a family member.

Usually dogs or cats are raised as companion animals.

✎ Vocabulary 이런 단어가 나왔어요

- 동물 animal
- 키우다 to raise
- 점점 more and more
- 늘어나다 to increase
- 예전에는 in the old days
- 함께 together
- 생활하다 to live
- 애완동물 pet
- 부르다 to call
- 즐거움 joy, pleasure
- 주다 to give
- 요즘 these days
- 반려동물 companion animal

- 많아지다 to increase
- 친구 friend
- 가족 family
- 존재 existence
- 뜻 meaning
- 보통 usually
- 개 dog
- 고양이 cat

📄 Learn More 더 읽어 보세요

Cultural Tip

While the Korean language does have separate words for dog (개) and puppy (강아지), more often than not people will use exclusively 강아지 to refer to both, regardless of the age of the dog. This has a lot to do with the fact that some of the harshest curse words in Korean have to do with the word 개. Other baby animals don't have separate names, they just have the word for a baby animal, 새끼, attached to the name; a kitten is literally "baby cat", "새끼 고양이", a duckling would be "새끼 오리" and so on. However if you were to refer to a puppy as a "dog's baby", you might get some very shocked looks!

26

택시 Taxis

서울에는 택시가 정말 많아요. 택시 요금은 비싸지 않은 편이에요. 기본 요금은 3,000원이에요. 요즘에는 택시를 부를 수 있는 앱도 있어요. 앱을 켜고 도착할 곳을 검색해요. 그리고 택시를 호출해요. 그러면 근처에 있는 택시가 와요. 정말 편리해요.

* 이러다 늦겠어: We are going to be late if we keep acting like this. ** 안 갈 거야?: You're not going? *** 걱정 마: Don't worry.

[서우레는] [택씨가]   [마나요]
서울에는 택시가 정말 **많아요.**

[택씨] [요그믄]   [아는] [펴니에요]
택시 요금은 비싸지 **않은 편이에요.**

    [요그믄]   [삼처눠니에요]
기본 **요금은 3,000원이에요.**

[요즈메는]   [택씨를] [부를 쑤] [인는] [앱또] [이써요]
요즘에는 택시를 부를 수 있는 앱도 있어요.

[애블]   [도차칼] [고슬] [검새캐요]
앱을 켜고 **도착할 곳을 검색해요.**

    [택씨를]
그리고 **택시를** 호출해요*.

    [인는] [택씨가]
그러면 근처에 **있는 택시가** 와요.

    [펼리해요]
정말 **편리해요.**

* 호출해요 is pronounced as 호추래요 when you say it quickly.

There are so many taxis in Seoul.

The taxi fare is not very expensive.

The base rate is 3,000 won.

Nowadays there is an app that can help you call a taxi.

Open the app and search for your destination.

Next, request a taxi.

Then a taxi that is nearby comes.

It's really convenient.

✏ Vocabulary 이런 단어가 나왔어요

- 택시 taxi
- 정말 really
- 많다 to be a lot
- 요금 fare, charge
- 비싸다 to be expensive
- 기본 basic
- 부르다 to call
- 앱 app
- 켜다 to turn on, to open (an app)
- 도착하다 to arrive
- 곳 place
- 검색하다 to search

- 호출하다 to call
- 근처 neighborhood, vicinity
- 편리하다 to be convenient

📄 Learn More 더 읽어 보세요

Expressions Related to Taxis

기본 요금 basic rate, basic charge

기본 요금 나오는 거리 base-fare distance

기본 요금 거리 base-fare distance

미터기 taxi meter

택시를 부르다 to call for a taxi

택시를 잡다 to get a taxi

택시를 타다 to take a taxi

모범 택시 deluxe taxi

콜택시 call-taxi

27

야식 Late-night snacks

야근 하느라 이제 끝났어 배고프다

저녁 안 먹었어? 치킨 시켜 놓을까?

치킨 좋아 맥주도 마시자

빨리 와 치맥 먹자

저는 가끔 야근을 해요. 그런데 야근을 하면 저녁을 안 먹어요. 저녁을 먹으면 일이 더 늦게 끝나요. 그래서 저녁을 먹지 않고 일을 하고 집에 가요. 그런 날은 너무 배가 고파요. 그래서 야식을 먹어요. 보통 치킨과 맥주를 시켜서 먹어요. 가끔 편의점에서 냉동 만두나 컵라면을 사 먹을 때도 있어요.

* 야근 하느라 이제 끝났어: I just got off work because I worked overtime. ** 치킨 시켜 놓을까?: Do you want me to order chicken in advance? *** 치맥: chicken and beer

[야그늘]
저는 가끔 **야근을** 해요.

[야그늘]　　　　[저녀글]　　　[머거요]
그런데 **야근을** 하면 **저녁을** 안 **먹어요.**

[저녀글] [머그면] [이리]　 [늗께] [끈나요]
저녁을 먹으면 일이 더 **늦게 끝나요.**

[저녀글] [먹찌] [안코] [이를]　　[지베]
그래서 **저녁을 먹지** 않고 일을 하고 **집에** 가요.

[나른]
그런 **날은** 너무 배가 고파요.

[야시글] [머거요]
그래서 **야식을 먹어요.**

[맥쭈를]　　　　　[머거요]
보통 치킨과 **맥주를** 시켜서 **먹어요.**

[펴늬저메서 or 펴니저메서]　　　　　　[컴나며늘]　　　[머글]　　　[이써요]
가끔 **편의점에서** 냉동 만두나 **컵라면을** 사 **먹을** 때도 **있어요.**

I sometimes work overtime.

However, if I work overtime, I don't eat dinner.

If I have dinner, my work finishes even later.

So I work without eating dinner and go home.

I'm so hungry on those days.

So I have a late-night snack.

I usually order fried chicken and beer and eat it.

Sometimes, there are times when I buy frozen dumplings or cup noodles at a convenience store and eat them.

✏ Vocabulary　이런 단어가 나왔어요

- 가끔 often
- 야근 overtime work
- 저녁 dinner
- 먹다 to eat
- 일 work
- 늦다 to be late
- 끝나다 to finish
- 집 house
- 가다 to go
- 날 day
- 배가 고프다 to be hungry
- 야식 late-night snack

- 보통 usually
- 치킨 fried chicken
- 맥주 beer
- 시키다 to order
- 편의점 convenience store
- 냉동 frozen
- 만두 dumpling
- 컵라면 cup noodles
- 사다 to buy

📑 Learn More　더 읽어 보세요

Cultural Tip

Koreans are very hard workers, and it is one of the reasons why the country has developed so quickly in such a relatively short amount of time. With such a strong work ethic comes lots of late nights and even working weekends. The hierarchy within Korean workplaces is very rigid, and workers are typically expected to stay in their office at least until their boss has left, which means people work overtime more often. Because of this, many people will not leave their offices until 7 or 8, sometimes later, even though they came in at 9am. This is also the reason why there is a separate word for late-night snacks, because so many of these hard working individuals wind up skipping dinner and instead have snack foods when they get home late.

28

동호회 clubs

동호회는 같은 취미를 가진 사람들이, 그 취미를 함께 즐기는 모임을 말해요. 정말 다양한 동호회가 있어요. 등산 동호회, 낚시 동호회, 춤 동호회 등등이 있어요. 보통 인터넷을 통해 동호회에 가입해요. 동호회를 직접 만들 수도 있어요. 동호회를 통해서 다양한 사람들을 만날 수 있어요.

* 코스플레이: cosplay ** 네 것도 있어: I have a costume for you as well. *** 스타로드: Star-Lord (from the movie *Guardians of the Galaxy*)

[가튼]　　　　　　　[사람드리]　　　　　　　　　　　[모이믈]
동호회는 **같은** 취미를 가진 **사람들이**, 그 취미를 함께 즐기는 **모임을**

말해요*.

　　　　　　　　　[이써요]
정말 다양한 동호회가 **있어요**.

　　　　　[낙씨]　　　　　　　　　　[이써요]
등산 동호회, **낚시** 동호회, 춤 동호회 등등이 **있어요**.

　　　[인터네슬]　　　　　　[가이패요]
보통 **인터넷을** 통해 동호회에 **가입해요**.

　　　[직쩝] [만들 쑤도] [이써요]
동호회를 **직접 만들 수도 있어요**.

　　　　　　　　　[사람드를] [만날 쑤] [이써요]
동호회를 통해서 다양한 **사람들을 만날 수 있어요**.

---

* 말해요 is pronounced as 마래요 when you say it quickly.

A club refers to a gathering of people who have the same hobby and enjoy doing the hobby together.

There are so many various kinds of clubs.

Hiking clubs, fishing clubs, dance clubs, and so on.

Usually you join a club through the Internet.

You can also create your own club.

You can meet various people through clubs.

✎ Vocabulary　이런 단어가 나왔어요

- 동호회 club
- 같다 to be the same
- 취미 hobby
- 가지다 to have
- 사람들 people
- 함께 together
- 즐기다 to enjoy
- 모임 meeting, gathering
- 말하다 to refer to
- 다양하다 to be various
- 등산 climbing

- 낚시 fishing
- 춤 dance
- 보통 usually
- 인터넷 Internet
- 통해 through
- 가입하다 to join
- 직접 in person
- 만들다 to make
- 만나다 to meet

📄 Learn More　더 읽어 보세요

Cultural Tip

Clubs, groups of people with a shared interest, are an integral part of Korean culture not only for young children but also adults. There are two words for 'club' in Korean: 동호회 and 동아리. The two words mean the same thing, but they have slightly difference nuances. If you were to hear someone talk about a 동아리, you would know that they are talking about a club at their school that is comprised of students. On the other hand, although 동호회 also means 'club', it is comprised of adults who are no longer in school. Another way to think of a 동호회 is like a meetup. If you were to say 사진 동호회 or 사진 동아리, both mean photography club, but you would know that one is comprised of adults with a shared hobby and one is comprised of students at a school who have a shared interest.

29

핸드폰 Cell Phones

저는 핸드폰을 항상 가지고 다녀요. 핸드폰으로 매일 음악을 들어요. 책도 읽어요. 검색도 정말 많이 해요. 길을 찾을 때도, 식당 갈 때도 항상 핸드폰으로 검색을 해요. 핸드폰 충전이 안 되어 있으면 조금 불안해요. 그래서 보조 배터리를 항상 가지고 다녀요.

* 드디어 완성했다: I've finally made it! ** 나는 스마트폰 없으면 못 살아: I can't live without a smartphone. *** 로봇: robot

[핸드포늘]
저는 **핸드폰을** 항상 가지고 다녀요.

[핸드포느로]   [으마글] [드러요]
핸드폰으로 매일 **음악을** 들어요.

[책또] [일거요]
책도 읽어요.

[검색또]   [마니]
검색도 정말 **많이** 해요.

[기를] [차즐]   [식땅]   [핸드포느로] [검새글]
길을 찾을 때도, **식당** 갈 때도 항상 **핸드폰으로 검색을** 해요.

[충저니]   [이쓰면]   [부란해요]
핸드폰 **충전이** 안 되어 **있으면** 조금 **불안해요***.

그래서 보조 배터리를 항상 가지고 다녀요.

* 불안해요 is pronounced as 부라내요 when you say it quickly.

I always carry my cell phone.

I listen to music every day on my cell phone.

I also read books.

I do lots of searches, too.

When searching for a place or when going to a restaurant, I always search on my cell phone.

I get a little nervous if my mobile phone is not charged.

So I always carry a spare battery.

✏ Vocabulary 이런 단어가 나왔어요

- 핸드폰 cell phone
- 항상 always
- 가지고 다니다 to carry
- 매일 every day
- 음악 music
- 듣다 to listen
- 책 book
- 읽다 to read
- 검색 search
- 길 way, road
- 찾다 to search for
- 식당 restaurant

- 충전 charging
- 조금 a little
- 불안하다 to be nervous
- 보조 배터리 spare battery

📄 Learn More 더 읽어 보세요

Expressions Related to Cellphone Charging

휴대폰 충전 cell phone charging
충전하다 to charge
충전기 charger
배터리 battery
보조 배터리 spare battery, power bank
콘센트 socket, outlet

30

냉장고 Refrigerators

한국에서는 김치 냉장고가 유행이에요. 김치 냉장고는 원래 김치를 보관하기 위해 나왔어요. 그런데 사람들이 김치 냉장고의 절반만 김치를 보관하는 데에 쓰고, 나머지 절반에는 채소나 과일을 보관하기 시작했어요. 그래서 새로 나오는 김치 냉장고에는 채소나 과일을 보관하는 기능이 생겼어요.

---

* 너무 더운데 '거기' 들어갈까?: It's too hot. Shall we go in "there"? ** 저기 진짜 시원하대: I've heard that it's really cool in there. *** 여기가 천국이네: This is heaven!

[한구게서는]
한국에서는 김치 냉장고가 유행이에요.

[월래]   [나와써요]
김치 냉장고는 **원래** 김치를 보관하기* 위해 **나왔어요**.

[사람드리]
그런데 **사람들이** 김치 냉장고의 절반만 김치를 보관하는* 데에 쓰고,
[절바네는]   [과이를]   [시자캐써요]
나머지 **절반에는** 채소나 **과일을** 보관하기* **시작했어요**.

[과이를]
그래서 새로 나오는 김치 냉장고에는 채소나 **과일을** 보관하는* 기능이

생겼어요.

---

* 보관하기 and 보관하는 are pronounced as 보과나기 and 보과나는 when you say them quickly.

In Korea, kimchi refrigerators are trendy.

Kimchi refrigerators originally came out for storing kimchi.

However, people started using only half of the kimchi refrigerator to store kimchi, and the other half to store vegetables and fruit.

So new kimchi refrigerators now have features for storing vegetables and fruit, too!

✐ Vocabulary 이런 단어가 나왔어요

- 냉장고 refrigerator
- 유행 fashion, trend
- 원래 originally
- 보관하다 to store, to keep
- 나오다 to come out,
        to appear, to be released
- 그런데 however
- 사람들 people
- 절반 half
- 데 for, on, to
- 나머지 the rest
- 채소 vegetable

- 과일 fruit
- 시작하다 to start
- 새로 new
- 기능 function
- 생기다 to be made

📄 Learn More 더 읽어 보세요

Types of Home Appliances

냉장고 refrigerator	토스트기 toaster
밥솥 rice cooker	청소기 vacuum cleaner
세탁기 washing machine	가습기 humidifier
오븐 oven	식기세척기 dishwasher
전자레인지 microwave oven	가스레인지 gas stove
전화기 telephone	믹서기 blender
선풍기 electric fan	에어컨 air conditioner
주전자 kettle	다리미 iron
정수기 water purifier	공기청정기 air purifier